HAPPILY

Also by Joan Aleshire

Litany of Thanks
The Yellow Transparents
This Far
Cloud Train

HAPPILY

JOAN ALESHIRE

Four Way Books

Tribeca

Please direct all inquiries to:
Editorial Office
Four Way Books
POB 535, Village Station
New York, NY 10014
www.fourwaybooks.com

Library of Congress Cataloging-in-Publication Data

Aleshire, Joan.
Happily : poems / Joan Aleshire.
p. cm.
ISBN 978-1-935536-22-2 (pbk. : alk. paper)
I. Title.
PS3551.L34779H37 2011
811'.54--dc23

2011027989

This book is manufactured in the United States of America and printed on acid-free paper.

Four Way Books is a not-for-profit literary press. We are grateful for the assistance we receive from individual donors, public arts agencies, and private foundations.

This publication is made possible with public funds from the National Endowment for the Arts

and from the New York State Council on the Arts, a state agency.

Distributed by University Press of New England
One Court Street, Lebanon, NH 03766

We are a proud member of the Council of Literary Magazines and Presses.

TABLE OF CONTENTS

HAPPILY: 1) by good fortune: FORTUNATELY, LUCKILY 2) *archaic* by chance: HAPLY 3) in a happy manner or state
—*Webster's Third*

For all my families

Finding a Story for My Granddaughter, Aged 3

Best audience one can ever have,
my granddaughter says, "Tell about
when you were little," settling herself
to listen in her little chair, all ears,
with the same trust she shows
on the street, putting her hand in mine.

"Don't *say* that to me," she'll say,
of platitude and lesson; she needs stories
with shape, but nothing to indicate
how happily spoiled I was, no sweet treat
denied me. I hesitate, in this small place,
to tell of the houses and grounds
that were mine to explore, safe
in a world her mother never knew.

"When you were my age?" she prompts,
patience stretched, and I find myself scooped
to the saddle of my grandfather's horse,
where I perched, many hands high,
my legs too short to hold me there.

Patient, the horse barely moved,
but I did, turning my head, and lost
my shaky balance, heading for concrete:
house, trees, cousins, groom, shouts spinning,
until the doctor searched my eyes
with his light and found me unbroken.

I bring back all I can, in the sun
of her attention, wonder to myself
what my parents feared and whom
they blamed, as she sits riveted
by this slip from safety, and safety
restored, with the smile of someone
who's just swallowed something she likes,
something that satisfies her completely.

1): *They loved fast horses.*

Larry Levis, Winter Stars

Catchlights: Angelica Peale

With held breath and a running start, I could escape
the wolves howling at cliff's edge, mountain lions
charging defiant stags, soldiers in fancy uniforms
killing one another in etchings that lined the upstairs hall,
but Great-great-grandmother's portrait hung high in the entry-way
surveyed everyone and everything—arrivals, departures,
deaths—her riverine eyes catching the light,
moving as her father had taught her brother,
who painted her late in their lives—
mouth drawn in a bow of disapproval
or missing teeth, her bonnet prim, tied tight:
a judge's hat, I thought, fleeing the stern gaze
that seemed to register my omissions and misdeeds.

In her father's portraits, a rose: a smiling girl,
dark curls abundant and tumbling (that old word
just right), blooming, before marriage took her
to a formal house, a husband who looked down
on her impractical father, her siblings named
Rembrandt, Raphael, Rubens, Titian, Linnaeus,
Sophonisba; their drawing room full of fossils
and birds' nests, pots of oil and turpentine,
well-smeared easels: all inquiry's glorious mess.

Exiled, she must have felt—not the first woman
entranced by a ruddy cheek, a certain vigor—
or thought a rich husband would be generous
to her family, and kind. Lodged in my mother's house,
now in mine, she seems more at home, her face

almost my mirror. If she judges anyone,
it would be herself. How she was at sixty,
her brother showed: solid, of her time, her class,
but with eyes alive, still catching the light,
keeping watch on what goes on outside the paint—
arrivals, departures, deaths, the cry behind the wall—
giving good counsel still, having seen so much.

Family Stories

Eating Susie, the children's pet lamb,
my grandfather began, "Oh, delicious Susie!"
and, at the tears, exclaimed, "What lovely duck!"—
which became the standard subject change,
cause of laughter down the years,
as if the Marx Brothers had written that childhood:
My grandfather changing to his bathrobe
and winding the clocks, showily, to show
lingering suitors it was time to leave;
and once, my mother stepping on his foot
when she slipped through a window after midnight;
or Aunt Betty calling her mop-like dog
"Guess" (which came out "Gueth,"
because of her lisp), so she could truthfully say
when someone asked, "What's your dog's name, dear?"
and keep them guessing, through *Floppy?*
Blackie? Rover? and *I give up!*
her *Gueth* growing more vehement each time.

Days of driving the pony cart along leafy roads
to meet Granddaddy's train at the local station;
times the ratcatcher arrived with a ferret
peering from each deep coat pocket—
a barrel of fun, I thought as a child,
envying that family, until in time,
other stories seeped through:
a mother often away or ill,
grandmothers dispatched to take the children
in hand, and the girl who would be my mother

answering all their commands and rules
with *I don't care,* and—finding her mother
resplendent in her hospital bed, pearls
dripping into the silk dip of her nightgown
as she flirted with residents and interns—
wondering, *Why do we visit*? and
Why don't you seem to be sick?

Nerve Cigarettes

My cousin hoped his mother wouldn't notice
the musty scent as they walked through the dorm,
but because the nose is the most astute organ
of memory, she lifted her head and straightaway
said, *Like Mother's nerve cigarettes,*
which is how we learned what Grandmother
loved: paper twists she'd slowly smoke
in bed, the silk kimono sleeve slipping back
on her thin arm to show the gold snake
whose jade eyes glinted as it clasped its tail.

The vise round her lungs would loosen
then, she'd enter the dimension
she felt destined for—acclaimed, adored,
sought for her beauty and brilliance.
With each inhalation, the house disappeared;
she was no longer an invalid, wife, mother of four,
nerves raw, but buoyed, as she saw herself:
rising from bed, bold as a queen.

Before

As she described it,
that summer was the hottest ever.
Two months pregnant, too sick
to eat, she lay on the porch
reading <u>The Pickwick Papers</u>,
which may explain my inclination
to laughter. She took pills
for the nausea, which may explain
my arms' inclination to the strange.

In the album,
at the beach, she leans back
on her elbows, stretches out
in a modest but revealing suit
that shows her thickened waist.
She wears dark glasses with
stylish light frames: carefree,
all our life before her.

Twelve Fairy Godmothers

all came with gifts to the birth:
one with laughter, one with strength,
one with luck, one with love,
one with grace, one with hope,
one with imagination, one with insight,
one with health, one with keen senses,
one with will, and one—
angry with the others or with
my mother, who didn't believe
in fairy godmothers, took half
my fingers, twisted both my arms.

Alive

The only sign on the *Certificate of Birth*
of something not quite right: the note
in an angular, stiff—unlike my mother's
generous, round—script: *Please Do Not Visit.*

And under *Trade, profession or particular kind*
of work done, as housekeeper, typist, nurse,
clerk, etc.—the only work women might do—
comes *Housewife,* in the same awkward,
unfamiliar hand. Under *Industry or business*
in which work was done, as own home,
lawyer's office, silk mill, etc.—which further
dates the document—the writer's put *Home.*
Under *Total time (years) spent in this work*,
she's written *Life*, as if she never was a child.

At the end, in the blank after: *I hereby*
certify to the birth of this child,
who was ________________, the writer's marked,
in a firm, round, close-to-my-mother's
usual script, as if her head has cleared
against the official world, her hand steadied,
Alive, this 18th day of March, 1938.

(From the Album, Not Her Camera):

She wouldn't have taken that
first photograph of me—a few days old,
swaddled in a blanket so neither hands
nor feet appear, lying separate, alone
on a floor in a triangle of light,
with shadows deep as black curtains
framing it on either side and almost
hiding the nurse-like figure who hovers
in a kind but helpless way nearby.
It's as if I'm being judged,
about to be left there.

Beginning

1.
As if in a dream, I know
how old I am, held in my mother's arms,
as she bends me close to Grandmother,
who lies in bed with the black machine
that hums, and cleans the air.
She'll say I'm *the smartest baby*
she's ever seen, slighting her own
children, and my older cousins.

2.
My mother marked the dates
carefully in The Baby Book:
when I sat up, crawled, stood,
said my first word, walked.
Also wrote, with terrible hope,
Her fingers are getting straighter.

3.
Nurse Morris pushed my pram
everywhere in every weather.
When someone too curious
leaned in under the bonnet—
And how is the baby?—
"And how are *you*, madam?"
was what Nurse M said.

In the photographs:

My face is always a sun
framed in clouds of curls;
my smile shows Chiclet teeth.
Who has ever seemed so
healthy, happy?

I lift my face to my father,
beaming as he crosses the porch
to my playpen and bends
to kiss me—too fast
for the dog lying beside me,
who leaps [the sequence stops here]
for his throat.

My mother has perched me
on the fence rail beside the road,
covering with her own
my smaller, weaker hand.
We look in the same direction:
at the distance that will draw me
one day away from her.

Three, perched on a porch-post,
my father's arm around me,
my legs dangling, surprisingly long,
I hold my first ice cream cone—
vanilla—with both hands.
With both—but holding it.

Maryland, Summer (Her Camera)

Pudgy in my jersey suit,
slightly voluptuous and entirely
self-satisfied, I dabble and lounge
at the edge of the canvas pool.

The boy and girl with me
seem in the snapshot to shiver:
thin, uneasy in the water.
I remember thinking, *Stiff,*
and *No fun.*

Their parents seem to me
so kind; why haven't they taken
the children out of the cold water,
wrapped in towels those shoulders
so tense with trying not
to shiver, complain, or
be less than the best?

If you'll ever get married

Clouds, dark blue berries
on the gum tree, no leaves yet
this verge of spring when I was
old enough to walk beside my mother,
when she walked slowly.
                                        This walk,
she said aloud—this once in our lives—
what she must have been thinking:
I wonder if you'll ever get married,
as if marriage were an award for looks
or good nature. She spoke idly, to the mild air,
not me, then covered those words
with others: all those I've forgotten.

Heads Together

We weren't aware she was there,
her step silent on the leaves,
the shutter the faintest click
that captured our backs—
sweaters' fuzz, Jack's shorn
blond cap of hair, the fine spun
aura of my tameless curls,
as we bend over something
the camera can't see—forgotten
now—that Jack found in the clearing.

The camera preserved us,
lit by sun in the shadowed glade
I thought an Indian camp or castle keep;
preserved his patience, care—thirteen
to my four—a boy who knit mittens
for his uncle overseas; preserved
his trust that I'd listen,
mine, that he chose to be with me.

A *snap* my mother would call it,
not fancy or deliberate, and yet
she saw our heads together,
crossed the dry leaves with care,
checked the light, focused, shot,

before we turned, saw the lens and smiled
into it, as we knew we were supposed to:
the spell of unselfconsciousness broken,
kept in a brightness not just of sunlight
around our almost-touching heads.

Three

Careful as she was, my mother must have
for a moment turned aside, stashing groceries
in the new '41 Ford's shiny green shell.
She must have been near, but I seem in memory
blissfully alone, the road stretched wide
and limitless before me—just a gas pump
and a few deep-porched houses in view then;
behind me the store we'd just left—
Anger's, though everyone smiled there,
weighing butter and fat chickens before the war.

It must have been days past my birthday,
because I began to say to myself, *I'm three,*
I'm three, as if this was the height of achievement:
no longer having to be a baby, *three,*
free of people fussing over my pram.
Three, the road invited me
to walk its length, wherever that was,
in an America that seemed limitless to me,
pre-war a few months longer, while elsewhere
Mandelshtam shook with fever in his dogskin coat;
Akhmatova waited in a prison line for news of her son;
Woolf in despair weighted her pockets with stones;
children lost their lives for being flawed.

I'm three, I whispered, not needing
to say it out loud, to anyone:
nothing to stop me on the Indians' path
due north from the Bay, walking farther
than my eyes or mind could see.

In No One's Family

Tag and laughter: a friend's daughter
darts away, singing, "*You*'re
not my grandma, you're nobody's
grandma!" and later when we ask
what she meant—her face in the back seat
calm in the streetlights' swim—
she says with no four-year-old's
assurance: "With hands like those,
she's in no one's family."

Her gravity takes our breath,
our speech—*Was this what*
everyone thought and never said?—
before we repair and reason.
Her voice—no hint of taunt—
has come from somewhere
beyond or behind her,
contradicting those generations
who made me not in no one's family,
but, happily, their own.

2): ... *a winter training...*

Hallowe'en, 1941

Wind rattled the shutters in their sockets,
but I was safe as I was snug, drifting
on wet leaf scent and woodsmoke
that came through the part-open window,
my chin at rest on the wide white cuff of sheet.
If I'd heard the bell, the crash, I'd have thought it
a stronger wind, and turned deeper into dream.

Lottie, who erased our mess and cared for me,
couldn't understand why the neighbors' FOR SALE sign
hung in the doorway above four figures in sheets
under the porchlight that became moons in her bifocals
as she looked up and the sign came down.
They gave her no chance to close the door against them,
slammed a metal edge against the forehead
whose brown smoothness made me calm,

breaking her glasses, gashing her temple,
where a few close curls escaped her straightener and pins.
Hit her as if she could feel nothing, or was meant
to be hit. Three sheeted shapes—and one
who later claimed he *tried to stop them*—
left the dented sign by the door, left her
without glasses to find the blood stains,
anxious to erase them before my parents came.

My father used the worst ethnic slurs
to describe his rivals, but never had a bad word
for anyone he called *colored*, and asked around in outrage,

until one neighbor's son came to confess, faltering
at my father's disdain. Balding, painfully correct,
forty years on, he'll pay his respects when my father dies.
I'm sorry, he'll repeat, as the mantel clock
measures another silence. Who am I to absolve
or blame him, I who left home believing I could
change things? What rose then on Hallowe'en
rises strong as ever. The metal sign called out,
irresistible in the shadowed yard. It clatters,
reverberates still in the stillness.

Waking My Sleeping Uncle: 1943

Out late with his friends on the steep ridge
above Dipping Pond Brook, listening to hounds
run foxes by moonlight—each bay distinct
in its tone—he'd sleep late vacation mornings,
until Grandmother lost her indulgence
and pushed me towards the mountain range
of blankets on his bed, trusting my guileless
five-year-old voice would wake him.
He should have hated all of us, who took
his last carefree hours, schoolboy dreams.

In months, he'd be just one more young
body in uniform, waking to cracked bugles
in dark barracks, then to the rumble
of Panzers coming closer, his feet close
to freezing, fingers clenched to his gun
in fingerless gloves, *hoarfrost glittering*
on upturned piles of dirt around the foxholes...
like being on the face of the moon
or being *part of that landscape...*

more alive than at any other time
*in your life...*on Elsenborn Ridge in the Ardennes,
reading Epictetus: *A corpse is your teacher*
and corpses are you, his comrades
frozen around him—out of the company,
alive: only two, making *the best of what is*
under...control—foxhole, canteen, gun.
A man must undergo a winter training,

as the Stoic said, even in absurdity—
the aunt who *must have been deceived*
as to the nature of the conflict sending him
a lavishly illustrated Upland Game Shooting.

Home, the man who'd begun *to hate the war*
slept with a .45, sensed snipers on every ridge.
No one dared wake him then; he woke
on his own, reading: *Heracles would never*
have become Heracles by slumbering away
his whole life in such luxury and ease.
What do you think Heracles would have
amounted to, if there had not been a lion
like the one he encountered, and a hydra,
and a stag, and a boar, and wicked and brutal men,
whom he made it his business to drive out and clear away?

Boars grunting *white traitor* at the schoolhouse door
and on the picket line; *boars* in the courtroom;
stags staking their claim to the ridgelines;
hydras to port and starboard; *lions* of illness
tearing their chunks of flesh. At his side,
a woman filled with sun. *Under control:*
focus, wit, a sense of the task to be done,
undergoing whatever could be under-
gone. And what couldn't be?
Undergoing that too, never less than awake.

(F.N.I. 1925-2007)

During the War

1. Overseas

The child in the story we didn't know then
keeps coming, swinging in her joy, being so
well able to move between her one good leg
and the crutch standing in for the leg
that's missing. The bell of her flowered dress—
the one with red smocking—and blue wool coat
hide the stump the cold air reddens and shrivels
as it bobs along. She keeps coming
out of darkness into sunlight, that falling on her,
fills her, sure in the lurch that doesn't seem
to her ungainly, being the only way she knows
to move, and she moves lightly, eager to show
the soldier who waits how well she can walk.
She expects he'll greet her with her parents'
delight, otherwise she wouldn't be upright and
smiling so, innocent of what's to come.

So I ran downhill to meet my father—
across an ocean and with two good legs—
holding flowers I was proud to have picked,
to hold, having partial hands, to bring
where he stood smiling, and took me in his arms.
The soldier waited to take the crutch;
before the girl fell, he seized her
by her good leg and swung her like a whip
against a wall. Or dropped her alive
in a vat of fire: like a scrap, imperfect,

a child my age in '43 or '44, much like me
squeezing my violet stems tight, believing
the world will greet her as she greets it.

2. The Duration

After the dream where the soldiers came,
they stood outside the bare bay window
every night—helmets, rifles, eyes
glinting in our lamps' light.
I held my breath to be invisible
on my way to bed, where I had to pray
If I should die before I wake,
repeating after my mother,
although I thought I *would* die—
the ceiling split with fire from the sky—
I pray the Lord my soul to take,
although I wanted my soul for myself.

If I screwed my eyes up tight, maybe God
wouldn't see in and find it. Was it He
or the soldiers who shone on my bed
the fierce light I tried to escape
by waking? The morning papers I learned to read
showed broken roofs like the ones I dreamed.
A town in Nebraska became a beach in France
where our troops were running and falling;
the forest where my uncle was was deep in snow.

The girl who crosses a station platform
in Poland on her crutch and one good leg
was invisible to us, who thought we knew
what war was—giving up butter, sugar,
Sunday drives in the country for what we called
"The Duration," while truth overtook us, in dreams.

3. Black-Out

The fire station went wild with sirens,
or a spotter warned my father—a plane
unlike ours had broken through.
Lottie and my mother knew to draw
the black-out blinds over every window
against the dark and the danger in it,
and hurried me to the thick-walled heart
of the house: the foot of the cellar stairs, far
from windows and outer doors. We'd wait
there the hours till *ALL CLEAR,* the three of us
in absolute dark, Lottie's starched-aproned breast
my pillow. In black-outs, what felt real *was* real:
mother's helper the earth that held us, or a tree,
my mother and I its nervous birds, praying
the scary bedtime prayer: *If I should die—*
and all the *God Bless*es: *my mother, father*
on his Air Raid Warden's rounds; *God bless*

his sharp eye for light escaping a blind,
his righteous rage when someone defied Black-Out.
God Bless all my friends and relations, and everyone
all over the world, except our enemies, the Nazis and the Japanese.

I swayed between consciousness and sleep, safe
between my mother and Lottie murmuring
above me, two women of one mind then,
hiding fear in front of the child they joined
to protect, until my father shone his flashlight
down the stairwell and told us the *ALL CLEAR*
had sounded. In the light, we were separate
again: lady-of-the-house, her maid, the child
who must go alone to her room. We were
the best, my father said, at Black-Out,
as if there were no differences between us.
Lottie brought milk to help me sleep,
not holding it to my lips as if I couldn't
hold it myself, but handing it so I could
take it from her fingers—strong, scarred
by little cuts and burns, purple against
the earth brown she was born with—
joining my baby-mouse pink, strangely
shaped ones around the luminous glass.

The Artist of the Dressing Table

My mother, her mother and sisters
all were effortlessly elegant,
so when one wartime winter's guest
sat in a slip at her dressing table,
I watched her treat her face
as if it were a canvas,
and she the artist of herself.

Plump, confident, five, I stood
just behind her, not leaning on
her, as my granddaughter does
on me, as she smoothed pale cream
into the hollows under her eyes,
brushed a faint pink onto pale cheeks,
made a red "O" of her thin lips,
drew her arched brows higher, blacker,
added black feathers to her lashes,
smiled, meeting my eyes in the mirror.

She finished with a feather puff's worth
of pink powder, then strong scent
went from crystal stopper to wrists,
ears, throat, lace-rimmed cleft
between her breasts, she saying nothing
more to me than pleasantries
in a voice made of whiskey and smoke.
What I studied, she knew she taught;
how to make of oneself something
else, not what one began to be.

Archival Footage: Johns Hopkins, 1944

Midway through the part where the hospital
congratulates itself—the surgeon the sun
in a constellation of cured children, grateful parents,
and one lucky dog who survived having her heart
torn and mended—a slim man in a long white coat
bends to a child's bed, putting his stethoscope
to her chest, then straightens, steps back
to greet his colleague, the expert
who'll change the child from *blue baby*
to pink one—and in his slim face, grace,
high forehead that inspires trust
I see—pause—rewind—play those frames
again—it has to be my father, vital and young,
called to test young lungs before the surgery
that brought so many there, while behind
these scenes, what made them so:
the surgeon's assistant who could never
become a doctor—being poor; being black—
but invented instruments fine enough
to thread through a dog's, a child's aorta;
invented the whole procedure, trying it
on the dogs first; losing most of them,
standing behind the celebrated surgeon,
talking him through every move,
while off-screen, orderlies scrubbed floors
and cages of shit and blood, ate, congregated,

eliminated in *COLORED ONLY* space.
Lost dogs unlucky enough to be caught
and brought here, had their vocal cords cut,
hurled themselves in a mime of howl against their bars.

The man not famous enough to be named
in the film, who may or may not have been
my father, stands a few moments, frames,
in the thick of his time—its worst and best—
reading a child's breath. Amid so much bad luck,
he seems lucky to be in this ward crowded
with pain and hope, and the child in good hands.

Packing-Crate Plane

My father wasn't one for tinkering,
hammering things, or mowing the lawn.
Bleeding the radiators of excess air
was his special chore, performed always
Sunday mornings, so as to miss church.
But during the war, when my love of pilots
was most intense, he built me a plane
from a wooden crate, not unlike the *flying boxcars*
he'd learned to fly in Canada at sixteen,
hoping to fight in the *First* World War.

No handyman, and not an artist,
but he saw the spokes of a propeller
in a bushel basket lid, a throttle
in a broom handle, an instrument panel
in a cigar box, to which he nailed bottle caps
just tight enough to turn.
For wings, he set one two-by-four
to starboard, one to port. For seats,
two boards more, nailed across the crate.

In flying weather all through the war,
my friend Diana and I sat in our crate on the grass,
imagining ourselves heroes, like her uncle Herb,
who'd joined the RAF—but couldn't know

what he knew: shot and taken prisoner, held
for four years; or what my father knew,
before he was my father, honing the habit
of holding in himself the terror
of hurling himself into thin air, and the joy.

FDR: April 12, 1945

My father, who knew how death
begins to mark a face,
thought FDR was *tempting*
fate, and shouldn't run again.
When the President died that spring,
my father was unsurprised, ungrieving.
My mother floated in flowered dresses
that floated about her, absorbed
in the new life that would be
my brother, mildly agreeing
with her mother, who called
"Franklin and Eleanor" *traitors*
to their class, although they were
too old for school; although
she and Eleanor could have been
sisters, sharing a taste in hats,
hairstyles, and dresses; and although
Franklin's *splendid deception* guided our lives.

Behind the pantry door sorrow
poured from the small box
that gave so much sound:
Swing low; Goin' home—
and Lottie and Bessie cried
without stopping or shame,
even though I stood watching

as they struggled to make our lunch,
unhinged by the loss
of a rich white man who reached
down from his seat of power,
acting as if it wasn't a wheelchair,
and drew others up.

The Barbells

Granddaddy's barbells stayed in his bedroom
after he died, maybe too heavy to move,
or left as proof how hard he'd been
wrestling weakness to the ground.

The clippings I found, poking in his desk,
showed him at the racetrack with a series
of women-not-Grandmother by his side
in tweeds and furs, grinning like big winners.

My favorite photograph of him, though,
comes from World War I: his bathrobe open
to his bare chest—a Man—with mud
at his feet and tents behind him.
What polio? his grin defies you to ask.
What weak leg?

Slow Down

Early March, it must have been—
racecourse fields hesitantly green,
brooks running swift in the deep cuts
of the Western Run, little green fists
on branch and bush—when she laid her hand
on his arm as he held the wheel,
and told him what she knew and had,
on her own, decided; told him in the car
my father loved for obeying him
so well—a '41 Packard convertible
that hurtled over bumps, around curves,
over the ridge separating their valley
from the one beyond. She sank low
in leather on the passenger side,
braced her free hand against the dash,
and said what he hadn't suspected,
"Slow down, or I'll lose this baby":
my younger brother just beginning.

My father must have braked, exclaimed,
held her hand hard for courage or luck—
that year the War went on, undecided—
to risk a difficult future with another
difficult birth, the prospect of imperfection.

Slow down, she would have said again,
but gently, as they sped together
into the future she chose: she who loved
horse races, and was still a fearless rider.

First Day

The first day of school,
I stopped outside, wouldn't
go further. My father was afraid
I was afraid. I couldn't explain:

I wanted to look at all the children.

At the head of the stairs, Mr. Brown,
head of the school, kind family friend,
took my left, better, hand in *his* left,
as I curtsied that first and every day:
Good morning.

Cold days, my father helped
pull off my thick leggings;
and those—he was always proud
to recall—of every other first grade girl
patiently lined up in front of him.

Taking the Stage

Tall for my age in first grade,
with a heft of excess weight
and self-importance, able to memorize
long parts and act them with ease,
I was perfectly cast as the grandmother
in the play I remember as being only
about Indians, though the Pilgrims
must have been there too,
to be welcomed to the country
and taught how to survive.

The Indians had, of course,
the best costumes—feathers,
beads and fringe for hunting
and dancing, while the Pilgrims
watched stiffly, dressed in gray.
My role as wise elder was central,
and so appealing I ran away with it,
playing shamelessly to the audience,
not noticing my grandson opening his mouth
to deliver his single line.

A shy, fat boy, nicknamed
by some well-meaning relative
Skipper, to give some lightheartedness
or captaincy to this child in need
of encouragement, he fled backstage
in tears, where in a flurry
of horrified mothers and teachers,

I was told to apologize.
Still in red make-up, headband
and fringed dress, I said the right
words as graciously as a royal leader
taking responsibility for an underling's mistake,
while Skipper snuffled and wiped his eyes.

Not sorry at all I hadn't let him
interrupt my unbroken dominance
of the stage, I thought him a huge
baby, and didn't let the thought
show, while his mother, mine, and our teacher
watched my performance with such
approving nods and relieved smiles
I was surprised not to hear applause.

Fire Drill

Lined up by grade, sex and height that first
postwar, not yet Cold War, year—before
the fear of atom bombs would make us
crouch under our desks—I stood near the end,
between *El*eanor, the tallest girl, and Elea*nor*
(who between them showed how hard it is
to spell in English)—when a child I'd never
seen before, who must never have seen me,
stepped from her place in another grade's line,
and stared as if I were something non-human.

What happened to your hands? she asked,
with an edge of blame, as if I'd chosen
to offend her sense of what was right,
and asked again as I tried to find a way
to explain what was to me, too, inexplicable.
On the offensive, she moved close,
violating the line's order and the decorum
we were bound, in line, to maintain.

Lost in my own ignorance, as I hesitated,
I was saved, by Elea*nor*, who drew herself
up like the great-granddaughter of a president
that she was, and said with disdain, as if everyone

should know what she was proud to proclaim:
"She was born that way," with such force
that the other, nameless child, retreated
to her own line and out of my life,
where I felt elevated by my own
difference, as if it were a privilege.

First Love

By first grade, I knew all my letters
and how to make them, but wasn't bored.
First, I'd watch Nicky—tall for his age,
dressed like a British colonial officer
in flannel shorts and ribbed socks
that never sagged, as he stood to recite
with the poise of a president, wearing glasses
that were, on him, unteasably distinguished.

Then I noticed Frank, who sat up front,
next to Miss Dye's desk, so she could
lean to prompt or pre-empt him
when he faltered—which was often—
or stared, uncomprehending, his eyes
an ocean's deepest blue, at Dick and Jane
or the blank spaces in his lined pad.

Which one should I love best?
Nicky made me think of gods,
who need nothing; watching Frank
try to make sense of words
that came as easily to and from
me as foot- and baseballs to him,
I imagined the hollow he must feel
at his desk: the blank I knew
in softball, trying to lose myself
in the outfield when a hit came my way.

When my birthday came, Frank
was the only boy I asked. He
brought the best gifts: riddles, jokes,
and complete attention to me.
Seven, we were engrossed in each other
through creamed chicken, peas, and rice,
through ice cream, cake, and wishes:
mine—that I kept to myself—
that we'd always be together.

The last day of school, Frank hunched
over his desk as the class rushed to leave,
wishing, I think, he could bob and weave
his way out of there, as Miss Dye
explained gently he'd be with her,
not us, next year: defeated by the words
I loved that played tricks on him,
turning upside-down and back-to-front.
I went happily on, not knowing I had lost him.

Christmas Angel

When the third grade chose me
to be the angel, they mistook
physical limit for spiritual reach.
They should have picked our newest classmate,
bravely injecting herself with insulin,
and golden-haired, blue-eyed besides.

Bossy, self-centered, yet I
was to stand, dressed in white,
winged and haloed, atop a book-case tree,
on which my classmates swayed,
waving ornaments and fringed green sleeves.

The structure I had to climb
shook as I climbed so high, shaking,
that the raised curtain brushed my head,
and shook as my classmates sang
and swayed energetically below me.

I tried to look as if I was ascending
into heaven, as angels do, except
that I was cross at the teacher
and trembling, ten feet off the floor.
If anyone envied me, they shouldn't have:
the burden of being good and prominent
so precarious, putting me above everyone,
that I prayed for nothing but a swift end
to "O Christmas Tree," so I could gain
the solid stage again: earth where I belonged.

3): ... *from nothing*

Learning the Birds

The winter pneumonia sent me to bed—
viral, my father said, *the best you can get*—
my mother taught the simple rules
of Parcheesi, which seemed grownup,
with its exotic name and the ornate
decorations of its board. But that game
took two; for times I'd be alone,
she brought new Nancy Drews—just like the old—
and my daily dose of schoolwork to do;
and fixed a feeder to the sill, to bring birds
to my window. And she gave names
to the red, black-and-white, blue,
brown-speckled, gray, and yellow feathered blurs
that swept in, stayed instants, swept off,
and fluttered in again. I learned to call them—
cardinal, junco, jay, sparrow, titmouse, finch—
lost the cough that had taken all my thought,
my self, to the wings' flash and stir,
to the watching and the keeping still.

"Prince Darius of Persia"

I had a director's tyrannical temperament,
which is why my playmates followed me
without protest, accepting the roles I assigned
in a play whose plot I stole from Shakespeare,
featuring rival princes, poisoned wine, and a queen
scheming for a throne. The cup intended for the prince
would have to be confused; in the end, everyone
would have to drink and die. I would play
the evil queen, and have the most lines.

Why our mothers gave us everything we asked for
is hard to understand: crystal goblets; a wedding veil;
as well as old curtains, satin mules, boas shedding feathers,
and a housecoat I could barely zip over my waist.
A concrete porch became the stage, where for one afternoon
we played to a patient row of mothers in lawn chairs,
and my baby brother wriggling to join in.
We knew the lines I'd written; we must have
rehearsed, but not enough to have blocked out
the action; at the end, there was hardly room
for all five of us to fall down and die.

The grape juice glowed, refracted by crystal,
the good prince drank from the right (for the play,
wrong for him) cup, his bride followed suit,
except that the cloud of tulle she wore
wrapped around the goblets as she fell, and had to fall
carefully, stifling her panic and laughter.

The bad prince and the maid, properly beguiled,
drank up, and collapsed where they could,
while I, the last to take a draught, acted as if
I'd escaped the others' fate, then grimaced
at the fatal taste, sank, and tried to fit my body
around the others already fallen, giggling, on the stage.

Just after the war: there had been photographs
of children's bodies heaped over one another
like this, but our mothers applauded politely
on the safe exurban lawn, and I appeared
before the curtain to thank everyone
I could think of: all who acted, watched,
lent goblets and the veil, still miraculously intact.
I thought of ever more ways to hold them: powerful
in their indulgence—that space where art
grows, though nothing I'd said or made *was*
art, only the possibility of it. I wanted
to thank even the dogs and the sky, the air,
for this freedom, to pretend, to be transformed
this afternoon, making something from nothing.

Poems That Every Child Should Know (1): "The Charge of the Light Brigade"

The little cat had no idea she wasn't a dog;
someone should have warned her, or me,
whom she followed everywhere—
Theirs not to reason why, theirs
but to do or die, as Tennyson said,
and like a brigade leader, I led,
proud, barely aware of her behind me:
black except for her white feet
and scrap of white chest; "Socks,"
I thought myself clever to name her.

We'd scarcely reached the lawn
when the real dogs, dark fur bristling,
set upon her, who had marched,
tail high, all innocence, up to them:
a little cat they tore between them,
as I screamed or stood soundless
and helpless beside them, and our neighbor
failed to halt them, until, in seconds,
all I could see was the bloody rag
of her chest tossed to the air.

My mother and our neighbor acted
as if Socks was just a cat—
casualty of her own stupidity—
and the dogs just part of a timeless

war. *Some rode back, out of the jaws*
of death, out of the mouth of hell,
but not, not the six hundred,
the poem went; but didn't say:
rode back not the selves who had
charged in, young, proud, and ignorant.

Sailing Class

When fog wrapped the harbor in gray felt,
we practiced our knots—clove hitch, half-hitch,
and the never-to-be-forgotten bowline,
for which *the rabbit went in the hole,*
and around the tree, and back in the hole again.
Or we learned to row; even I—though I
couldn't hold the oars tight enough—
sat with one of the teachers, knee to knee
while she pulled the dinghy through water
still as glass, in circles, going nowhere—
an enlightened solution, but awkward
for us both: I ashamed to be unable;
she unable to find words to make it
less obvious, or: make it go away.

But some days the best sailor in the Fleet
came down the gangway out of the mist
with his sailbag slung over one shoulder,
balancing the hump he was born with,
making his own weather; heads turned
not by his body's difference, but his skill
as skipper who attracted the best, best-
looking crews, and was envied by the rest,
until his chest caved in from the weight
of his hump; his heart, having given its all,

gave out—all his life the champion,
steering his craft so close to the wind
it skimmed the water ahead of the rest,
and he was one with wind, out of his body
or only this: eye sharp to the full sail.

Artificial Ones

Ten to my nine, L impressed me
when we first met, flinging herself
from her bike, playing dead.
When I didn't cry out
or run for her mother,
L grinned, got up;
I'd passed her test.

In sailing class, she always chose me
as crew to her skipper, and once,
as I threaded the jib before a race,
the girls in the next Bullseye
asked L, not me, "What happened
to her hands?" Looking up the mast,
as if to find the answer there,
L said, "Oh, she'll get artificial
ones when she grows up,"
and I gripped my strangeness
hard, to feel the pulse in it.

Chasing Fire

Summer of brown ferns and alarms—
the island half ash from the year before—
my oldest cousins would speed off
when the village siren groaned
three long groans for fire, and come back
older, more important, smoke in their hair,
telling of treetops that burst into flame
above their heads, though it was never clear
what they did besides watch there,
clothes, hands, faces still clean.

I found my chance one day
at a single groan, didn't wait for three,
crouched in the back of Jack's car,
trusting he and Jim would look nowhere
but where the flashing lights went
until they reached the circle of engines,
tankers, pick-ups parked every which-way,
men digging a fire-break and the fire
leaping it, snapping and hissing out of a pinetop
above our heads, drawing me out of the car
to see the blossom of fire, men bent to work,
lifting soot-smudged faces
towards Jack's new red Chevy coupe,
its white walls and canvas top unspoiled.

They paused to stare at the rich summer kids
who'd brought a little girl along—*Did they*
think this was a picnic, for Chrissake?
In the heat of their collective rage,
there was no arguing with Jim's clench-jawed
We have to get you out of here,
as he propelled me to the car,
while Jack rolled up the sleeves
of his Brooks Brothers shirt to show
his good intentions, both brothers knowing
they'd be blamed, not me, as if they
had lured me into that heat, sweat,
danger, work: that heart of the real.

Before I've figured out

how to take the coins,
the storekeeper drops the change
from my first purchase
past my hand, which is
stretched as much—not
much—as I can stretch it;
and laughs as two quarters,
dimes and a nickel ring
on the counter and I
scrape them up, flushed,
furious. What kind of joke
is this, that leaves me
out of the laughter?

Off-Key

The way you wear your hat,
the way you sing off-key...
"They Can't Take That Away From Me"
George & Ira Gershwin

After I sang alone in front of the class,
Miss Wright pronounced the sentence
Tone-deaf with a relish on her sharp red lips
I *wasn't* deaf to; her pinched pale face,
stretched, I thought, by the permanent wave
that turned her hair to wire, seemed incapable
of pleasure. Something had gone wrong
with her hips or jammed her legs into her pelvis;
what had happened to her I never knew,
but the fierce energy of her commands—those, too,
I wasn't deaf to—the short, stubbed steps
she took on short legs, and the hitch of her strange hips
as she aimed for the piano bench, indicated pain.

Unlike the other women who taught us
with the dedication and abnegation of nuns,
she seemed, with her precise red lips
and heels high as stilts, to defy the stereotype
of spinsterhood, pouncing on each of our flaws
with the vigor of negative enthusiasm.
In place of the unselfconscious
happiness I'd had singing, she consigned me
to mouthing, hiding in the back of Chorus,
and a class meant to help the tone-deaf, in which
she struck the keys of the tinny assembly-hall piano,
and ordered me to match its notes, a task as performable
as flying, my vocal cords strangling in shame.

And so for years I was silent, avoiding
hymns and group sings: mute as if music
were a language I never could master, not even daring
to raise my voice in the shower's muffling rush, until
this very morning of my life, when a letter addressed *Dear Abby,*
asks nothing of that sibyl, makes no complaint, but seems
truly meant for me, written by one Ralph Emerson,
with all the clear assurance of his famous probable ancestor,
having sensibly eliminated the now-comic middle name.

Nobody, my Ralph writes, out of the blue
and into my salvation, *who can speak*
is tone-deaf, and no one should tell a child
he is. The feminist and editor in me
would change *he* to *he or she,* and wonder
why *Nobody* and *no one* are in the same sentence,
but I read on: *Many of my students have thought*
they were tone-deaf because someone told them so
when they were children.

Miss Wright, who found her pleasure
in our faults and childish transgressions,
who excluded me with such certainty from singing,
was actually wrong! Fifty years ago, so it's unlikely
she's around to read this, which would make her
old age more miserable than it undoubtedly was.

Revenge,
            though, isn't what I want; it's
singing, which I was doing all along, just
off-key, which, as Ira Gershwin reminds me
this same morning on the radio retrospective—
The way you wear your hat, the way you sing
off-key—might actually be its own kind of ON.

Mind and Matter

Dreaming, reading, happily eating
like a Gilded Age tycoon, I lived
somewhere beyond my body,
unaware of my size and shape,
until a summer sitter's small-boned speed
and sharp tongue made plain I was
elephantine, and *in the way*
as she flirted with our cousins' tutor.

In photographs I was as broad across
as Great-aunts Frances and Jane,
who loomed in yards of crepe de chine.
My arms by contrast seemed spindlier,
stranger; I didn't argue with my parents'
You have to put your mind to this.

The diet doctor had unforgiving scales,
an ice-blue, ice-pick stare I couldn't fool,
diaries to fill with plain and tasteless foods,
and a *you-can-do-it* confidence I couldn't
disappoint. I looked for pleasure
in dry toast and thin blue milk; found some
in the metal counters shifting left
on the scale; and in the mirror:
the hint of a cheekbone, the dent of a waist.

Our Father's Forehead

for my brother

You thought you could never live up
to him—perfect athlete, physician—
but if you'd been old enough to see him
then, to know he'd been gone all night,
you'd remember how his face shone,
erased of every expression but the light
that stunned him as he bore it
towards us: our mother swinging you
in the swing hung from the maple
overlooking the field—when we swung,
the ground dropped away under us—
and I, eleven, not playing: reading
a difficult book, wanting my reading noticed.

Gods of our world, our parents moved
through our childhood in the grace
of never being questioned, never being wrong.
And our father especially was used
to being right, saying the words
that would save someone: seeing the flaw,
germ, wild cell, and knowing what to do.
And so, when he came across the grass
to us that Sunday, close to noon,
he seemed to stumble, blinded
by all he'd had to see:
a friend struggling all night
to give birth in an iron lung.

Nothing to be done for her: mother
of three girls already, one my age and friend.
I don't remember the words he used
to tell us; I knew the ending from his face.
He couldn't hide the truth; his forehead
shone with it. Something more powerful
than all his skill took life, though life
shuddered all night in the balance—
oxygen pumping into the glass coffin,
the surgeon swift to no avail.
Something else worked more swiftly,
invisibly, surely, out of reach.

If you had seen him then, absorbed
as you were in swinging, in being
only four, you'd have seen he wasn't
as godlike as he seemed—dispensing
Thou shalt not's: as in *Don't be*
so goddamned temperamental,
or *Don't be ridiculous* at some
childish outburst of mine—
this father so far above us,
his shadow absorbed ours,
his stride put him so far ahead
we could never hope to match it:
to walk beside him, talking of nothing,
or something important, as he bent
his shining forehead down,
and we could confide in him, unafraid.

Poems That Every Child Should Know (2): "In Flanders Fields"

A poem the old book said every child
should know, I did, by heart, loving
its predictable rhymes and regular
iambic tetrameter: *In Flanders Fields*
the poppies grow / Between the crosses
row on row / That mark our place....

The abrupt mid-line halts and inversions,
reversals and delays stand out now
in their strangeness: *That mark our place;*
(here I kept saying *graves*) *and in the sky /*
(the shift that almost took my breath away)
The larks, still bravely singing, fly,
Scarce heard amid the guns below.

I thought *Flanders Fields* was one small place,
not acres of graves; didn't take in
what the poet meant by: *We*
are the dead. Short days ago,
We lived, felt dawn, saw sunset glow—
a man who'd spent seventeen hours
covered in blood, bits of flesh and bone,
saving scarcely any of the wounded;
and of those saved, leaving none,
including himself, whole;
a man who sat on the tailgate
of a bloody ambulance, scrawling

on an unused script for morphine
the careful verses that were the one thing
he could do at that moment, then lost faith
in that too, crumpled the scrap
another found and saved, which is why,
out of hell, we have it, and children
used to have to learn it by heart,
before they could grasp the haunting
the poet foretold: *We shall not sleep,*
though poppies grow in Flanders Fields.

But Pat, Limping

Gun-shy, a retriever bred for the hunt, unfit
for the work, terrified of thunder, too, trembling
in the farthest closet corner he could squeeze into,
given to my grandfather, whose soft heart
brought other strays our way, the dog
would have been shot—his worst fear
brought right to his head—
and not come to be *Pat*, our guard
and companion, not afraid
when the task was protection:
lunging one morning at my father's throat
as he bent over the playpen
where my face rose to his kiss.

The dog would have given his life
for me, if his chance to be heroic
had come; as it was, he faithfully put
the verb *to dog* into action, with us
its direct objects, part of the comfort
we took for granted: broad curly head,
brown curly fur to be patted
absent-mindedly, until a delivery truck
turned too hard in the narrow drive
and struck him for his attention.

Unset, his leg drew up as if his body
was trying to protect it, and withered
into an almost graceful shape.
On three stiff legs, he limped, propelled

by his strong chest and stronger heart,
surging behind the new puppy
meant to replace him, determined
as I was, that summer's hottest days—
sweating, crashing my mother's pre-war
two-wheeler, hauling up its metal bulk,
trying again and again for balance.

I had no problem in 6th grade that fall
with my "most unforgettable character"
composition, describing Pat in precise detail,
in contrast to the younger dog gamboling free.
I'd begun to love the way I could make words
obey me; closed with, "But Pat, limping
on three legs," and a clause about triumph—
lost now to embarrassment—that made the class
cry as one, while I stood by tearless, thrilled
by the hinge *But Pat, limping* made,
between loving the dog, and knowing
I could use him.

Freedom of Speech

Free of her, and old enough to laugh,
we repeated the incident none of us
had seen, but none disputed—the plot
so probable, so satisfyingly true
to the facts as we knew them—
that one day Mrs. B flew into a rage
fiercer, even, than her habit, over some child's
failure or mistake, and stamped her small foot,
shod in the pointy-toed, spike-heeled pumps
she favored; stamped like Rumplestiltskin,
until her ankle broke under the weight
of her impotence. A woman who had no
choice but teaching grade school,
or believed the small can be controlled,
she was everywhere in our small world—
tutor, overseer, director, commander, coach—
with no classroom of her own, able to swoop
down—Tennyson's *eagle like a thunderbolt*—
on our flaws: black eyebrows, red nails, sharp
eyes, nose, toes, hair permanently controlled,
everything about her honed to an unforgiving edge.

As if we were all in training for the C.I.A.,
she oversaw the maps we traced of ancient empires;
perched on our desks, tensed for closer
inspection, she pounced on unpromising executions—
mine with its blurs and blots of revision.
Her scorn even then seemed absurd:
maps weighed lightly in the scale of grades.

I had no fear when I found her
the coach of 6th grade graduation,
where I was chosen to recite.
Eleven, self-important, self-confident,
I loved to take the stage, and said
from memory in my usual style
the rhymes I'd been assigned.

Silly, simple to remember, easy
to say—a *jingle*—I thought I'd done it
perfectly at rehearsal, and was amazed
when Mrs. B commanded me to do it
again, but differently, stressing the syllables
she would stress, changing the slow
cadence of back stairs and kitchen,
repeating the stupid words, which she
had probably written, until I could make
no sense of how I *should* speak,
and took the flower-banked stage
at graduation queasy and trembling,
for the first time terrified to speak.

I said the verses as if my mouth
had forgotten how to move, sure only
I'd remembered and uttered them aloud,
believing my voice and way of speaking
unalterably wrong—and so for years I shrank
from speaking to groups of more than three—

miserable class president, heart and stomach
in revolt—until the Sunday it was my turn
to lead school Vespers. I dreaded the chasm
that always opened as I rose from my seat,
but found the words I'd chosen—Common
Prayers, the sure repetitions of the King James,
coming through my mouth, as if I were only
the means to the utterance, and my body,
my voice with its particular sound
and rhythm, had dissolved into the broad
river of speech I at that moment so
wholly believed, I trembled at its force.

4): ... *all you can*

Hard of Heart

Years after I could do it myself,
my mother washed my hair.
Twelve, thirteen, naked in the tub,
I sat obedient under the suds
and spray the winter day
we heard from deep in the house,
through thick walls and muffling floors,
an ominous bang, before the water lost
its warmth, the radiators stilled.

To hear my mother's lament,
her fear, one would have thought
the house in ruins, us without a home.
Shivering in the tub, oblivious
to her emotion, I said coldly—
I *was* cold—"Just call the repairman,"
which only made her angry,
as well as afraid. *Hard-hearted,*
she accused me, who *didn't understand.*

We were far from poor, and could
always stay at Grandmother's, I argued,
righteous, hardening my heart
indeed against her unreason,
not knowing how much order
and beauty were her bulwarks—

to be built carefully, maintained
constantly—against the memories
of childhood: sudden dramas,
departures, the house neglected,
no grown-up there to trust.

Fingers in the Bread

Hardly the food revolt in "Potemkin"—
no bugs in the gruel or historic implications—
but the impulse to resist was surely the same
the day the lunch consisted solely of soggy
corn fritters, Karo syrup, iceberg lettuce,
cream cheese balls dredged in peanut butter,
and piles of bread: squishy white loaves
dumped carelessly out of their wrappers.

I can't recall what made us all
start laughing instead of complaining
or leaving the room; what made us
start throwing the cream cheese balls
at one another, until someone thought
to hurl them at the light bulbs and ceiling.

Then Sallie and I were drawn to the bread,
those toppling loaves, pushing our fingers
through the unresisting mush, laughing,
punching holes in all the loaves in the room,
schoolmates egging us on, and falling away,
noticing before we did—so absorbed
were we in joy—teachers hurrying in
from their own lunchroom, in alarm.

Sallie laughed as I couldn't remember
her laughing since her father died.
Good girls, top of our class, we shocked
everyone except the head teacher,

avuncular Miss White, who reminded us
properly of waste and world hunger,
yet managed to convey amusement,
even a kind of approval. We were thirteen,
not sorry, though we pretended to be:
giddy from the first fight in a revolution.

Bad Taste

Usually one headmistress played bad cop—
Miss M of the huge hands and feet,
man's haircut and heavy signet ring;
the other played good—Miss O, plump
and fluttery as a dove, cooing blandishments
and fancies. Both, though, acted as one,
with disapproval and disdain, rejecting the script
I'd written for the 9th grade play.
In bad taste, they said, as if my words
were spoiled: sour, smelly, immoral.

The rules of etiquette then
were clear, and constantly repeated:
Keep your elbows off the table;
your mouth closed when you chew;
knees always together (at least girls').
Please and *Thank you* should be
as natural as yawns, but yawns
themselves should be suppressed,
along with fidgeting and—God forbid—
picking in public one's teeth or nose.
Once when I burped and apologized
for burping, a teacher said I should *NEVER*
say that word again, so that was in bad taste, too,
although my father always said it.

The rules of good taste were embodied
and implied by my mother: what she wore,
bought, and said of others: *What a SHAME*

she won't lose weight! Why doesn't she do
SOMEthing with her hair? No one
in my play would wear tight clothes,
burp, chew gum or pick their noses;
why did my script so offend?

A mild spoof of "Star Trek," an exercise
in silliness not based in Greek myth
(favored by Miss O) or the Bible (beloved
by Miss M), shaped by the common currents
around us, long before the barrier between
good and bad taste was irrevocably broken;
long before I'd take pleasure in breaking it.

Canter

A torrent of muscle lunging under me:
the horse lurched forward, I lurched
back, squinched, perched, precarious,
the saddle no help in the rush and bump
of this genteel gait short of a gallop
I must *master*, declared Mrs. Whit,
who believed her Christian Science:
that mind triumphs over matter;
insisting I have horsemanship
in my veins and must try every day
to ride as well as my mother.

No matter that my mother, her father,
older sister, younger brother all
meshed to their horses like Centaurs—
in the ring I was put in,
bars I had to clear, gripping harder
with shaking knees, exposed
to the sharp commands, *Head up,*
heels down—terror made me brave
enough to resist, no matter that if
I wouldn't be her pet project, her
miracle, I'd lose afternoons like that
last one in the barn: the sweet horse-
sweat smell as I curried damp fur,
the stall private and golden with dust,
the warm animal stalwart to lean against,
as I watered and grained her, felt the graze
of horse lips, grace of a velvet nose.

Falling off the Roof

Hiding our horror of what would come
to all of us—the bright blood-bloom
against the white of N's underpants
when she straddled the seesaw unaware—
we mocked the first among us to fall:
Fallen off the roof, gotten the curse: disgusting!

We mocked the shadow of shaved hair
in A's armpit, played Keep Away
with her deodorant, mimicked the shape
of her breasts—*just like grapefruits,*
we said, none of us wanting to be
women, if this was what *woman* meant.

The book every mother gave us
only said *the stork didn't bring you*,
and offered illustrations, as if we were made
of upside-down hourglasses, leafy branches,
and nests brimming with eggs.
The blunt tubes and pipes of male anatomy
could have nothing to do with us.

I wanted to be free forever
of womanly straps: the confining belts
and bulky pads my mother stocked
for the day I, too, would fall
off the metaphoric roof, waking
to a rusty stain in the crotch
of my girlish, clownish polka-dot pajamas.

If anyone told me habit
would soothe encumbrance and inconvenience,
I wouldn't have believed them.
No one would have said how salt-sweet
my own blood would smell—
evidence I was like others:
stained and fallen into life.

The Man Who Looked Like Henry James

Sent to the dance with everyone thir- or fourteen,
in high-necked organdy that emphasized
my innocence, too young to be conscious
of myself, not sad or ashamed to be just
watching the dancers from the porch,
dim in lantern light—What did the man
who stepped out of the crowd towards me
see in my unformed, unfocused face?

Barely taller than I, bald with a fringe
of dark hair, no one I'd seen or would ever
see again—poor houseguest or heir to a fortune—
he kindly moved from the shadows to invite
what must have seemed the neediest child
to dance to one of the standards even I
could dance to. The art of making conversation
from nothing was one I hadn't yet learned,
but he went straight to what he intended to say—
You'll be beautiful and famous some day:
prophecy I marveled at, never forgot, lived
as if it were true. As if he were the spirit
of Henry James, whom I later believed
he resembled: James, writing a friend:
Live all you can; it's a mistake not to.

Least Favorite Babysitter

To be fair: I haven't forgotten
the addictive taste of the butter cookies
she made every Christmas.
To be fair: I probably would have hated
anyone my mother hired to babysit
my little brother, and me by extension.
Fifteen, I argued, was old enough
to take care of an eight-year-old,
or call for help if help should be called.

But Mrs. S. gave me other reasons
to hate her. Folding clean clothes,
she'd hold up a scrap of elastic
and lace meant to hold up or in
the new weight on my chest,
giggle and bray in her thick German-
American, "Here's your BRAY!"
as if she'd made a great joke. "BRA!"
I'd snarl, but she never got it right,
or didn't want to, kept mocking
my pretensions to femininity—the way
her village ancestors might have thrown
turnips at the hunchback, the dwarf;
laughed as their missiles struck home.

Pillow Books

In the little books I was given each Christmas—
padded plaid or leather, puffy as pillows—
I wrote about the day I drenched myself
in so much perfume before dancing class
that Flo's mother said, *WHO is wearing all that*
Arpège? and shamed me for thinking
such a cloud of grown-up scent
would make all the boys dance with me,
not just fat Sammy from my bus
and loud Scotty who loved his pet snakes
striking their glass cages with their fangs,
gulping the wiggling mice he threw them.

I wrote what I'd never say: *Z looks like*
Heathcliff in his black coat with the collar up,
sad (and more handsome) because his team lost,
in love, everyone says, with E, who makes out,
everyone says, with every boy who asks her.
No one will ever ask me, *ever love me,*
I keened with the strangely satisfying self-pity
of thir/four/fifteen, overrunning the lines,
the limits of each day's space.

Why was I born? I asked the universe
in my stiff, back-slanting script:
all I thought and could never say
to anyone but the little books that accepted
unacceptable truths without comment
or concern. Because they kept their secrets,

no one would suspect I was less
than carefree, cheerful, perfectly
satisfied, having absorbed the lessons
my culture taught—*Never complain, never explain;*
Think only of others—all the while sure
no one had ever been like me.

Purity, Circa 1954

Cloistered girls with little to do,
we gathered Saturdays at one house
or another, gossiped, played Charades,
board and other games: once—
and only once—the *Purity Test*,
whose point I grasped was not
to be pure, unsought-out, un-
done to; the winner won
by answering the most questions
Yes: *Have you ever been*
kissed? French-kissed? Whatever that
was, I laughed along with the rest,
the empty laugh of not getting the joke,
hoping a parent would intrude
before the questioner got to me
with *Have you ever gone*
to first base? Second base?
Third? All the way home?
Wherever that might be;
had any of us gone there?

My neighbor shifted,
smirked, proud to win points
for *Yesses* all the way to second base.
Could I count the brush of F's lips
on my cheek when we were seven,
or the cold sandpaper scrape
of the face opposite mine at T's birthday
when the bottle stopped its spin?

On the spot, pinned, flushed,
I could, *had* to, lie the ten points
past the shame of undesirable
zero, blended again into the circle
of girls ordinarily my friends,
as beside me, X hesitated, choked
on her *Yes*—embarrassed like me
by her innocence, I thought,
when I was too innocent
to imagine any other reason.

Point of Order

Thick walls, soft rugs, no voice raised—
We were cushioned, cocooned by ease and grace;
the world's clamor barely reached us,
the house itself a point of order, except
when the forces of disorder broke
from the small screen with a snarled
POINT OF ORDER! *POINT OF ORDER*!
and drove my mother from the room,
pinned me—self-important, fifteen—
and my father in our chairs to watch
what might be disorder's undoing.

Orderly, moderate, my parents
had no fear of being called disloyal,
but someone they knew had been,
for knowing too much about China.
What repelled my mother, riveted us.
Chaos spoke loudest and seemed
by sheer repetition to win;
the face of madness—real
before us—grew craftier, bolder,
its pocked skin whiter, eyes,
stringy hair and stubble darker,
until the patient judge
looked over his wire-rimmed glasses
and asked the way God should
the question that wasn't a question
that restored order to the house, the world:
Have you then no decency, sir?

Pizzas

Never having heard it said,
my mother pronounced the word
PIza, as in the Leaning Tower of;
PIza, she was proud to say,
to be up-to-date, mid-Fifties,
but what she served my friends and me,
my brother and his, for lunch
those Saturdays she'd call *the happiest days*
of her life was nothing like the pies
slid from Little Italy's ovens—
this suburban approximation
she'd found in *Ladies' Home Journal*:
English muffins topped with American cheese
and tomatoes, run under the broiler
with, maybe, oregano, surely no
garlic, but surely delicious, satisfying
tastes not yet hungry for the exotic,
the distant world that would draw me
so far from this comfort.

I turned away as easily
as I pushed back my chair, as if home
were merely the wall of a pool
to launch myself from, swimming—
not that table arranged
for my pleasure, and at its head,
my mother's hopeful look
as she filled our plates.

Her Art

My art teacher says I have lots of talent!
Letter from Paris, 1929

Nudes and fruit—the former more
awkwardly rendered—student sketches
from Paris one winter, and art school,
tied tight in black portfolios, attic-held
until I found them, signs of a dream
she never mentioned, saying only
of the *atelier*, *how cold* it was:
the drafty, light-filled space
where she held the charcoal too tight
until she learned how broadly, finely,
shadingly it could move, her hand
coming closer to the right proportion
of pressure to freedom, almost,
not quite, putting on the page
the grace and weight of flesh before her.

Nothing exceptional—finishing-school art—
except that she who gave or threw away
anything old, unused, unsightly, out-worn
kept so many examples of it—fond relics
of the life she'd left behind—
as every day she brought her family
flowers, ease, light, fine food,
and immersed herself, selfless, in the art
she didn't choose, wouldn't have
chosen: harder, more subtle, original—

brave—being not *from life*, but *in* it:
doing what no one she knew of
had done before, raising as usual
a child different from the others.

House Afire

We got along like a house
afire, my father would say: *Afire*:
straight ahead, without a hitch,
as flame buoys a hot air balloon;
not *ON fire*: as in something
you never want to see.
Afire, the Orioles played their best,
their first day in the majors,
with my father and brother cheering,
then coming home to an actual *House*
ON Fire, ours: the roof erupting in flame.

Until the alarm, that Thursday
was dull, like all Thursdays;
I'd stood in my slip, dreaming,
supposed to bathe and change for dinner,
imagining I was Eva Marie Saint
about to kiss Marlon Brando—
and for once, threw on clothes
without thinking how I looked;
felt, for once, part of my family,
helpless, shocked, as distant sirens
wavered closer, minutes expanded
to seem more than minutes,
while my mother and brother cried,
my father cursed, and I kept quiet.

It's a tragedy, my mother insisted,
wringing her hands next day,
and I was too young not to argue:
family, friends and neighbors hadn't
hesitated to empty the house;
sofas, beds, lamps, tables and chairs
drifted on the lawn in new configurations—
all saved as the firemen attacked
the attic floor with hatchets, found
a layer of asbestos that stopped the fire
and seemed a builder's brilliance then.
All saved, as the moving van a brilliant friend
had called arrived ahead of rain.

All of us—I pointed out the obvious—
saved, well-housed and -insured;
what was *tragic?* Of course, I'd
spent the night at a friend's, free
to borrow whatever I wanted,
entertained at dinner by the daredevils
who'd led the charge to save our things—
getting along, I didn't say, *like a house*
afire. I didn't ask if the great rush of help
wasn't like that too, or why it couldn't
buoy her, set her, like me, afloat.

Like Hemingway

When his mother married the baron,
he talked, I thought, like Hemingway:
of drinking Aquavit, and hunting chamois
in the Austrian Alps—

After the races, still in his silks
and redolent with sweat—his own
and his horse's—he yanked open
the passenger door and shoved in
next to me, growling, *Move over,*
Beautiful, while N, who drove,
and L, in back, chastised him,
rightly, for rudeness, and I
basked in his presence—shoulder, thigh
against mine—thinking, *He treats me*
like every girl.

Grandmother's Gifts

At seventeen a shallow girl, serene
in my assumptions, never needing
questions or explanations—
different from my schoolmates only
in the unmentioned twist of my lower arms,
the number of fingers—at Christmas,
when my parents made sure all grantable
wishes were granted, I found the cashmere cardigan
de rigeur among my friends, black
as I'd requested, wanting to look serious,
intellectual, grown-up; and Eliot's
Complete Poems and Plays, whose rhythms
I'd repeat under my breath in study hall,
instead of the assigned Pope, Wordsworth, and Thomas Gray.

From my grandmother, rich in every way
but health, nothing I imagined wearing
then: a slip of peach silk that felt
like another skin touching mine,
rimmed in ecru lace that barely
covered the bodice and the high slit
at the hem: a garment suggesting a bed,
a dim room, the moment before an embrace,
leading my parents to complain of Grandmother's
extravagant and inappropriate gifts.

It would be years before I took that slip,
for a lover, from its tissue-paper folds,
and longer still, no longer so serene

in my assumptions, and curious
to know my young, incurious self,
that I took from the shelf her other gift
that year, that seemed even less
meant for me: a slim book emblazoned
with red letters on a black ground:
Karl Shapiro's Poems of a Jew,
a name not among those I was learning
to admire. Why this? A title so blunt,
a cover so brash I was embarrassed.
Was Grandmother hinting at origins
that our family—familiars in the halls
of privilege—had so far concealed?

Serene in my assumptions, knowing
not to ask questions, also a snob,
I never read those poems Shapiro said
were *not for poets*, didn't think I needed
to know those *letters of Jews as strict*
as flames, until I found "Mongolian Idiot":
    Pity and fear we give this innocent
    Who maimed his mother's beautiful instinct
and "The Leg": *He learns a shape*
                That is comfortable and tucked like a sock.
                ...The amputation becomes an acquisition.

Blunt truths we never mentioned,
there on the page I never looked at
until I'd become no longer so serene
in my assumptions, blithe in my impressions,
and could turn to my uncle with the social tone
I adopt to hide feeling, "What a great reader
Grandmother was, how amazing she gave me
Karl Shapiro," at which my uncle cast
over his glasses a laser look that asked
without asking how I hadn't understood
her gifts all along. I must have been
just a blur to him, as he shone his fine
searchlight down the halls of our past.

A Self

If all we are, and will be, we are
at eighteen, we look in the class picture
like three rows of policewomen-in-training,
in our blazers emblazoned with the school seal
that read, in Latin, *To Be, Not To Seem*,
our hair uniformly short, close to the head,
save mine that veers out, but only a little.
What made me *me*, part of that time, place,
class, acting with no consciousness of self,
being a different self, who followed the rules:
Do unto others, Think only of them,
moving ever forward, looking neither back
nor *in*, wrapped in the obliviousness
I was born with: a happy accident of birth.

Sought and unbidden, memory and albums
give glimpses, until in the reunion book
come snapshots that seem new. Can this
be me with the long legs in baggy shorts,
cradling a daschund, the only dog I've never liked?
Me dressed in Sunday best and beaming,
in a strange headband-hat? Me after graduation,
my smile uncomplicated by disappointment,
although I hadn't won the English Prize?
Me in a rush of enthusiasm: a girl
of impossible innocence, strange to me,

and familiar, drawing me to her:
this earlier self an ancestor to be
lived up to, as she moved that June day
through the hot gymnasium, arms full
of blue ragged robin flowers; white organdy,
the most guilelessly beguiling of fabrics, crisp
and translucent, below a sweating, shining face.

5): ... *like childbirth*

The Elvis Argument

began in a cave of blankets and sheets,
at the far end of my parents' house,
my radio tuned, low, to the high-voiced
early rock that sweetened my homework too:
Dream, dream, dream; Donna was her name,
and the thrill to be found on Blueberry Hill
in my first rebellions and the boys I'd share them with
in the throbbing hallways of Heartbreak Hotel:
loves I'd hide decades from my mother,
until the summer night, lulled by wine
and rare soft air, conversation slow
with three generations at the table,
I made the mistake of mentioning "Mystery Train,"
a favorite of mine and my daughter's,
and worse, the mistake of summarizing the plot
as "two Japanese teenagers besotted with Elvis,"
which stirred my mother's slumbering resistance
to that "disgusting cheap actor," whose
cultural importance my daughter and I then
rushed to establish, until my mother snapped:
"But Elvis was *common*!" and we cried as one,
"But that's the point!" and my daughter took
her rage to the night, while in her wake,
my mother sat confounded by the loves of her own
flesh and blood: all that had escaped her
fierce attention streaming in invisible waves
through thick covers and walls to reach us.

Astray

My mother seemed in those days possessed
of an unassailable sense of right, never
hesitating to tell everyone (in the family,
at least) what was wrong with their hair,
their housekeeping, drinking, clothes—
Are you going out in THAT?—and beliefs.

Home from freshman year, I hadn't begun
to dress like a beatnik, hadn't chopped off
my hair; my resistance to church confused her.
Summer afternoons when we took tea,
looking like ladies out of Edith Wharton,
she'd begin: *You don't believe in God?*

And I, fresh from Hum 2, "Good and Evil
in Western Literature," in love with Camus
and his cigarette, would answer: *What kind of God
lets innocents suffer?* Which would bring her
so near tears, I'd lie: *I just
want to share what I've learned,*
then couldn't resist a jab: *I love it there.*

Which brought from her the worst curse
she could think of: *What are you anyway,
an agNOStic? All those Communists in Cambridge
have led you astray!*

There, finally, was a way
to agree: *Agnostic, yes* and *Oh, yes, astray*—
but there was no answer to her *What happened*
to you in that terrible place? How could I
have let you go?

Tree of Life

The rug's reds would have been
clearer then, closer to blood,
the greens grassier, more redolent
of spring, the blue more like a northern summer's sky.
The pattern would have been easier
to trace from trunk through angled branches
to petals of cream and rose, springing up
in profusion and at random.
No real tree would be this orderly,
but women with small fingers and children
permanently bent to the sight-stealing work
did their best. The Tree of Life's alive

on my floor. Would anyone have studied it
as I do, through the grit of my carelessness
that darkens it between sweepings?
My father's desk rose from its island once,
afloat on a sea of polished parquet,
smooth as untroubled water, or ice.
Patients who could afford his skill
would face him there, anxious for his verdict
on a tremor, flush or pallor, after he'd probed
a neck's Braille with his fingers, pressed
a balsawood wing to a tongue, bent
his silver receiver to bring blood-
and breath-sounds to his ears.

Fearful, stoic, oblivious, sicker
or sturdier than they knew—all of them,
equally poor before him, would learn
the mysteries he'd found inside them.
The heavy desk shone, a coffin
set across the Tree of Life on the floor,
but a leaf would curve out, a clutch
of petals release a lily's scent
into the room, where my father,
who believed hope the best medicine—
though he was no believer, and had missed
the tumor in his best friend's brain—
would say, "It's a perfect picture."

Or he'd point to the shadow
that changes forever
the picture, the room, a life:
the blur that makes him say,
"Medicine is two-thirds mystery;
we'll work together," his firm hand
warming the patient's chill.

The Tree of Life has tight buds, and blossoms
that defy definition, branches that end
abruptly and ones that seem endless,
growing through the design, around its rim.
The weavers set some flowers free
within the form, taking in the loose,
lush shapes rare moments of pleasure.

The patient, with so much life underfoot,
wants to believe my father: *The best medicine*
is hope. Her world askew, future uncertain,
cast off from health, still she floats;
bobbing wildly, still she doesn't sink.

My Mother, Reading

Not the right choice—raiders, *reivers*, outlaws—
A terrible book! she says, although or because
we descend from the most prominent thief.
Terrible! she flips to the title page,
as if unable to believe anyone could write
about such villains, let alone publish the same.
Awful! but she reads on, in the intent monotone
that once let words come to life on their own:

> *The trouble with all Anglo-Scottish wars*
> *was that no one ever won them;*
> *they were always liable to break out . . .*
> *There was no future for a Borderer*
> *. . . trying to lead a settled existence . . . .*

She reads on, as absorbed in this book
she doesn't like as in those she does—
about lives lived well, with no bad ends,
no poverty, eccentricity or pain.
Hard books to find—fluff would insult her—
and I find them with difficulty,
so she can read with the fine new lenses
that replaced the cataracts, fixed
on the page in worlds freer, bolder
than her own, where people move
at will, as she can't now—runner, rider
that she was: no raider or *reiver*,

though their vigor has come down to her,
who shuts out whatever she can't accept—
me correcting her mistakes, asking questions
whose answers she's forgotten—as she
holds her book: her shield, lamp, and sword.

Lost Name of the Lost

There's no one left to ask, of the ones
who might remember, so I'm making up
the name of the dog my mother loved
and left, out of love and unknowing.

Kerry, I think she called that Irish setter,
making up a name that sounds right,
the way she'd invent events
to hide her failing memory.

He was the most beautiful dog,
she said all my childhood,
and his red-gold feathery coat,
his sweetness lived beside us.

What she never said, until she
was on the verge of leaving:
she left him with her family
when she married and moved away.

Her new yard was too small,
the streets and leash too harsh
for a dog who'd always run free,
she reasoned, but the dog,

of course, didn't understand
reason, only her presence, then
absence, and lay at the door
of her old room, not moving
from the long dark hall.
Kerry—not eating,
not raising his head for anyone.

The Last Mirror

Other women at the salon envied her
her thick silk hair, the fineness of her features,
the sure hand that made her eyes larger
in their mascara frame, her cheeks' rose,
mouth delicately etched with lipstick
she used like a wand, her gesture intrinsic
once learned, like swimming or riding a bike,
smoothing the tomboy edges,
embracing the womanhood of her day.

Taking an hour to dress: the perpetual
slowness that maddened my father,
who liked to be everywhere before he was due.
A turn now to the patient nurse: *Do I look*
all right? and long minutes of jewelry box
decisions: which earrings, necklace, pin
to wear with the housecoat she would put on
the last night she would come to the table,
amazing us; she'd hardly eaten in days.

Hastily we lit candles, made our portions
smaller on the best plates, and stood
as she rolled in in her chair, waving
like a queen to us, her subjects.
In her lap she held, and fingered
with one hand as she ate, her largest purse,
deep as a horse's feed bag, brought as if the trip
from bed to dining room would take weeks.

Afterward, pulling the drawstrings apart,
I found her staples: gold lipstick case
like a bullet; square of translucent linen,
her scent on it; silver compact that enclosed
a goosedown puff with pink powder-grains in it,
a latched compartment half-filled with caked powder,
and in the lid, the last mirror she looked into.

Like Childbirth (2002)

I always wanted everything clean
and pretty around me; I wanted
my body to be pretty and clean,
she says as Kim cleans
the body that isn't.

I don't want you to be here!
"She means *you,*" Kim says to me.

Mr. Dirk could do a great job
with this; she pulls with surprising strength
on the hair that falls forward
as I lean over the bed.

I can't think of anything more
I want to do with my life.
Later: *Why can't I*
just die ?

I don't want to go out
screaming [words from a movie
she saw in the Thirties?]

This is like childbirth:

[the hospital bed, her legs bent
against the pain, nurses attending:
a labor that brings
something to completion.]

I remember when I first saw you...
I said, "You can't, you mustn't.
It's my child...."

I loved life [*loved* stressed, and in past tense]

I don't want you to cry—
My forehead's pressed to the bedrail;
You should go out and have some
fun....

[Where could I be,
but here? What kind of fun?]

The pain patch seeps in:
Where's Dad? [Dead years ago]
Grandmother Cook and Aunt Jane
are coming through the light plug,
the one in the corner: There.

[Dave and I are laughing, but looking...]

I was in a dark field...
I felt as though
I was being stretched...

You are my light...
My new life
began with you...
[The one she wanted?]
I wish you were always here...
[I who've always argued, determined
not to be like her?]

On her birthday:
You are speaking out of life...
[What did I say?]
Fingering the daffodils
brought from the old house:
I think I've done everything
I wanted to

Coughing, the next-to-last day:
Life is HELL!

Poor child, rubbing my bracelets;
I loved them exactly
the way they are.... [My hands?]

She'll never say
who said she should keep me home,
just that someone *had.*

Half-asleep, and hot to the touch,
the next-to-last night:
I'm going home....

Tuesday morning,
as I turn to leave:
Do you HAVE to go?
[as usual]

"I'll be back soon."
[but it won't be soon enough.
It'll be Sherma
who'll say in her soft Island voice,
Just let go, like a midwife urging *Push.*]

Clearing the Room

Her bedroom has emptied of all that was
here, all that was hers—the most ordinary
and the most intimate things: the bed she lay
and died in; the chest that held the flimsy silks
she wore next her skin, the curtains and chairs
upholstered in roses; the spindly desk
that held its secrets fifty years—
the folded note *I'M SORRY I WAS BAD*
in my brother's crooked crayoned caps,
(Was he five? Six? What had he done?);
my letters of delight at being on my own, away;
and one from my father, when I was eighteen,
not stamped or mailed, clearly delivered
by hand—by a man, as she said,
who *didn't like to talk*
about feelings, and wrote:

Dearest,
You've done a superb job with Joan—
I who didn't understand she was
working, didn't know how hard.

Descendants

Seven, Ixcanil may not remember
herself at one-and-a-half, as she walked
with the pride of beginning walkers,
straight to her great-grandmother's bed,
undeterred by white hair, wrinkles or the aura
of final illness, and said unprompted
the name family and friends used
for my mother, "Hi, Peale," as if
to someone her own age, delighting my mother,
then slipping into her final week.

Seven, Ixcanil remembers what we've said
more than the old woman reaching out
her blue-veined hand—*Sweetheart*—
but sitting close in her maternal mode,
with no trace of one-upsmanship,
she tells her little sister, "It's too bad
you didn't know Grandma Peale,
Nik'te'. You would have loved her."

Acknowledgments

Thanks to the editors of the following journals where some of these poems first appeared, sometimes in slightly different versions:

The American Scholar; *88: A Journal of Literature* (Hollyridge Editions, 2006); *Victory Park:* A Journal of the New Hampshire Arts Council.

Thanks also to the editor of the anthology *Never Before* (Four Way Books, 2003) where "Fingers in the Bread" first appeared.

Special thanks to Martha Rhodes for pushing me to go farther and to the community of writers in the MFA Program at Warren Wilson College for being a great audience.

Notes

"Catchlights: Angelica Peale" is for Andrea Barrett. Angelica Peale Robinson was the daughter of early American painter Charles Willson Peale.

"Archival Footage" was inspired by the documentary, "Partners of the Heart," and the book, Partners of the Heart: Vivien T. Thomas and His Work with Alfred Blalock: An Autobiography, by Vivien T. Thomas.

"Off-Key," "Freedom of Speech," and other poems of elementary school are dedicated to my fellow alumni of Calvert School in the 1940's and '50's, especially John Waters.

Joan Aleshire was born and grew up in Baltimore, Maryland. She graduated from Radcliffe/Harvard in 1960, and from the MFA Program at Goddard College in 1980. She has taught in the low-residency MFA Program at Warren Wilson College since 1983, and lives in Vermont.